LEDA'S DAUGHTERS

"*Leda's Daughters* pays homage to a wide array of figures and scenes from Black and Native histories. Sometimes K. Avvirin Berlin mourns the violence of these histories, at other times she points to moments of creative fugitivity. But always and throughout, Black and Native bodies escape the forms of narrativity that have confined them and explained them and they make a leap, through poetry, into opacity, truancy and love."

– Jack Halberstam,
The David Feinson Professor of the Humanities, Columbia University
Author of *Wild Things: The Disorder of Desire* and *In a Queer Time and Place*

Leda's Daughters

Poems

K. AVVIRIN BERLIN

2023 Jean Feldman Poetry Prize Winner

Washington Writers' Publishing House
Washington, D.C.

COVER ART by K. Avvirin Berlin, 2023
COVER DESIGN by Andrew Klein
BOOK DESIGN and TYPOGRAPHY by Barbara Shaw

ISBN 978-1-941551-34-9
Library of Congress Control Number: 2023940456

Printed in the United States of America

WASHINGTON WRITERS' PUBLISHING HOUSE
2814 5th Street, NE, #1301
Washington, D.C. 20017
More information: www.washingtonwriters.org

ACKNOWLEDGEMENTS

"I Am the Fugitive Daughter of Your Eyes," "Orion Women," and "Pilot, 1935" appear in *The Iowa Review*.

"Love Root: Atlanta, 1881," "Lakota Grammar," "Atlantic Crosses," and "Iphigenia at Birmingham, 1963" appear in the Winter 2021 edition of *The Georgia Review*.

"Shadow Feast: for Sojourner Truth" and "John Brown's Body" first appeared in *Boston Review Online* on January 31st, 2020.

"Discuss.," a semifinalist for the Adrienne Rich Award, was printed in *Beloit Poetry Journal* in Fall 2019.

"Wild Flag" was published in *Women's Studies Quarterly* in the Fall of 2018.

CONTENTS

Mama 1

Dig Me Out, *or* Lot's Daughters on the Auction Block 2

Even the Fishermen 3

Saint Joan of Harlem 4

Orion women 5

Discuss. 6

Shadow Feast 7

John Brown's Body 8

After Moonlight 9

After Woolf 10

Scavenged Thing 11

Shroud of Kateri 12

Atlantic Crosses 13

Grace Came for John Newton 16

Girlhood and Its Sorrows 17

The Mermaid of Charleston, 1867 19

Love Root: Atlanta, 1881 20

Declaration 21

We True Truants 22

I am the Fugitive Daughter of Your Eyes 23

Harlem, 1912 24

Some Ellen 25

Ally 26

Pilot, 1935 27

It's Hard to Explain 29

Work 30

Dilate. 31

Untimely Ripped 32

Gone to Ninevah 33

Pie 34

Phaedra's Love 36

Leda's Daughters 37

Helios Child 38

Iphigenia at Birmingham, 1963   39
Pax Animalis   41
The Haruspex   42
Wild Flag   43
Helen of the Swamplands   44
After Her Eyes   45
Backbone of the New South   46
The Widow's Oil   47
Shared Crop   48
Pearl   49
The Sounding Field   50
Lakota Grammar   51
After the Flood   53
Vivarium   55
Ruin   56
Inhabit   57
Aureole   58
Amen.   59
Be My Body for Me   60

Mama

On a darkened stage she calls "Mama?" Mama, I want your skin.
Then the animal that is mother steps into the light and sings.
Both clothed in white, they are one beautiful bone
but Mama reeks and retches, opens her mouth
and is a child sold

to a century sated only by song. Songs sweet, songs slung
in satchels over the backs of women workers, songs slipped
past the stiff necks of men whose wives rubbed the roundness
off their own souls, then had children so like them that
they are one unbridled bone.

Dig Me Out, *or* Lot's Daughters on the Auction Block

"take my dark daughters. do with them
as you please. only
don't lie with the angelic flesh of men,
however willing it be."

Lift my skirt and I will bare my teeth.
Lift my skirt and see
the divine animal
dressless—
unblessed.

Even the Fishermen

Like smoothing down the corners of a bed;
everything right. new again. the brain after its lapse into injury:
that time you tried to climb (foolishly; it was only the third story)
to the furthest reach of things, where she whose blood you share
stands, half-laughing, her mind a place too muscular—
for even the fishermen
their wild haul.

Saint Joan of Harlem

Let there be horses
and torches

so the armored Saint
may ride, illuminated

past 145th Street and Broadway
to the waiting river.

And her mother may say
(as she did then)

"My daughter followed the instructions of God
to the best of her mental abilities."

And the Church may at long last
say Amen.

Orion Women

for the women of the Great Dismal Swamp

Enter SHE, song stitched, forty, first found singing in a swept kitchen, child on her weeping knees
like some please-prayin' woman wandered miles from her home in the mud stuck swamp.
SHE could live nowhere tilled, tiled or shined, nowhere lustered or lean. Just give her
the swamp: wind gusts, mean gamblers, Orion women who possessed rich folks' round
eyes in squishy pockets, measured the length of their days by whiskey shots, were desired
and despised by men who laughed, "you jezebel witch of a woman, how much money do
you have in the bank?" Knowing *none*, then spit, spanked gleeful knees

who could not see the deep cherishing that arose in her cheeks as SHE beheld
her daughter, born of thick water and a midwife's skilled hands, this July 1853

who saw charity, cheap thrill, another woman done run, a wonder SHE was not killed...

not the cat that plodded through the mess of the living to visit her each day, who
brought her gifts of small owls and once, a swan, still alive, black as her daughter's
newborn eyes.

the swan she kept on a length of rope just *so,* knotted so the winged thing would not leave
her baby's cradleboard (as they were friends now, and betrothed).

By 1870 SHE was bone.

Perhaps the stage will resurrect her, perhaps the swamp will bear her back, for how could
SHE who'd walked the length of the wild world not

"Want to be kissed like I am wanted. Want to be alive again."

Discuss.

A. If, in the 19th century, young girls buried their dolls in mock funerals, did black girls too? In no more than 3-5 pages, or 2,500 words, wonder: did black girls name their dolls Christmas Come Early? Must they have made their dolls themselves from the discarded husks of corn at shucking time? With pushpin eyes, could they, too, see the sky? Was this the harvest? The blue of it? Despite the whip?

B. If, at the start of the 20th century, couples commissioned photographs by which to remember their deceased children, in posthumous states of play or repose, and if their children, as a result, appeared doll-like on the plate, were such photographs of black girls commissioned too? Or were black girls thought too enfleshed for the frame, forgotten? If forgotten, consider by whom. Not their God, certainly? For He was listening. Perhaps by the fields of juniper bushes that had failed to hide the girls from the bared teeth of the white woman for whom they labored, her ordinary anger. So that they'd been exposed when she called as they hurried away down the tree-lined road that day, and could only like muted dolls, stay.

C. And yet they were very much alive. There is today a room teeming with dolls of all shades who gather at night, consider their plight, "If, in the world of objects, each of us is merely a 'thing among things'[1] how to sing our anthem? How to bring our bodies back from their boxes, or, worse still, from the places they were simply left, unburied, bereft: a depression in wet ground; between the metal limbs of the cotton gin, behind the master bed after his sin"

D. Where he didn't know I'd hid.

---

[1] Frantz Fanon, *Black Skin, White Masks.*

Shadow Feast

for Sojourner Truth

Filament of layered light littered on the plate: a photographic triptych to behold: the stark Quaker garb you adapted in the early 1860s (black shawl, white skirt, cane whittled as an awl) draping your three poses. Gone then the wild days of the '30s when the white girl lay abed with you as the Prophet did her, kissing you all over after you'd both removed your shoes, her marveling at your height in the night's hailstorm. With he who called himself Prophet away in the city it was alright; all the birds were starlings and you considered less your son Peter's fate, that he played dice with those Irish boys and assumed that dignified Negro's name when cops asked why he was out late. Peter, now gone and ghosted in the hulls of a great ship, a seafarer writing you letter after letter knowing full well he could have done better, knowing as well you cannot read, and would not reply anyway with Ann—fakefrail and flailing—the one slipping neat nails through the neck of his letters, simpering at you as if she did not sip from the syrup of your black body on rain-lit nights.

John Brown's Body

[Antigone and her blue-uniformed corpse.
Come dawn, and carrion, Creon crawls North.
You are bastard and brother both,
pestilential Polyneices.]

Islands of washer women, working free, fucked in all matters civic, yet favored by the gods, float
on foot, having felled the house that bound them. Singing what your body became, they converge
on Union camps, hum, shoulder each other like wedded wheat bared to sun—kin to them who'd
walked, run guns the day of the raid, when you, God-crazed, stalked the federal ferry in VA. "*He
has gone to be a soldier in the army of the lord*" they tell those who will hear. Marking their
music, your graffitied hanged-man's body, which "lays a' mouldering in the grave" greets what
it sees in the watchfires:

Antigone and her union north.
Alienesque, blue-bodied, torched.

After Moonlight

"Who is you?"
she what made you calls broad your name.

At long last you are and were: a boy at the horn of plenty.
mouth of a man now-well-past-twenty

Trills, "oh you, oh Black oh blue oh oracle tell
of the gills by which you breathed these long years."

Sand-caressed, he was what you erected in the water's stead,
the only man on this side of the Atlantic who still calls you by your shine.

You are my friend. You with whom I rested on linens fine.

When the Atlantic parted he returned to feed you parboiled rice. He'd taken other lovers,
fattened them up real nice.

And here was the music that the tendons stretched over your bones like a harp bow
had played for a decade. Here it was on the jukebox and him just standing there looking

For what you are and were: every orifice and oracle of your skin that retires the sun. And you
undone.

After Woolf

She in her red dress with her hunger somehow still, and no one to claim her where she lays, a musical moratorium. Ridden with the usual ills of the poor, but bedecked in crimson, she displays the problem of the female vagrant: that there are too many cities to love and they give their love away so easily. That they come in droves in excess of men, walk bold as brass up main streets. That they must be studied, assessed for their essential quality of living: to wake up each morning, the mind a whole animal slaughtered according to one's own precepts, and say "yes." Too, too lovely their laughter; lewd, lascivious, loud as passing thoughts— "What a life I've not lived." For, their ribs and ribaldry, their hips and hope, bespoke burdens to you unknown. (You'd said blithely, "Can't you tell it's burning?" when first asked for your hand. And now you were not even _____ anymore but Mrs. _____, picture of feminine frivolity; flowers on the table not the table of thought itself.) But vagrant women, working poor, were free as they fashioned themselves. Fabled and sometimes failed, they found one another in want ads, shared spaces large and empty, not *a room of one's own*, but a hallway littered with many hearts that, together and apart, beat the *unsolved problem* of the poor poetess. Big hearts, beggarly hearts, hearts that beget other hearts, hearts that shout, *call me any other name you please!* to those who, in pale penitence, toss stray coins at penures. You/we/I from whose mouth[s] lies flow, we fictive women, bodies of work by one another towed.

Scavenged Thing

for Harriet Jacobs

— to see — to stitch—
them winter clothes, I snatch an hour from the wailing load.

Today marks seven years of Christmases.   God masquerades as mistresses.
plaited tresses whip   painted lips warn   "I'll make a lady of you yet."

Dress damp with vigil,
she scampers away as daylight flays.

Night grins bright, flint-sharp teeth scavenged. I, ravaged
seethe with my grandmother's glory; gleam and glint. Regent

of broken places
cast over
a body in a moat I
try to forget his hand on my throat.

Grace floats, guides me to those who trespass north:
water-black men who bring abolitionist prints and ribbons for my daughter

       Ellen (sweet as heaven, not yet sold). I have since sewn her woolen coat,
made a blanket hewn from the sinew of animal. Beneath it I dream of me,

       A seafarer who dares leave, passing myself darkly. My body, sailed, assailed,
holds fast to whatever wind set it flying at the mast. Onboard I cast my hope

             Onto detritus: days that dawn for us the damned.

Shroud of Kateri

for Kateri Tekakwitha (1656-1680)

This was not the first time you'd seen them, black-robed

men wearing small, gleaming pendants in the shape of

So you were bold enough to rise and say to the frozen earth, "bear fruit."

And there was Eden.

Not in some far-off place, but in Kanawakhe. Not in any other time but now.

So you said farewell, bound your hair and breasts, blessed your mother's grave.

Travelled to the Frenchmen's town where you, a nun, were forbidden

the wisdom of *wampaum* to wield against disease and guns.

All around were lives smallpox had claimed yet you,

scarred, stared unafraid at towering steeples.

Bride of none. Saint of a people.

Atlantic Crosses

for Pocahontas/ Matoaka

1637

Thomas, flowering with tobacco leaf
Atlantic crosses, arrives
at the confederated river.

You remain in Gravesend, buried.
Though near here lies
Your festering child.

1617

London is frill and fancy built upon a groan
Girlishness does not become you, and you are slow
becoming, reluctant to nestle into the fold of fabric that settlers set and sew.
You contort instead into a shape remarkably like grace, comfort
your wailing babe born
on the shifting Atlantic.

The River Thames
Is so unlike the river in your veins.
Cargo captured crowds and crows: a
bonneted burnt brown woman
clasps the pale hand of a boy,
Cranes her neck.

Look again.
This, too, is water.

"Surely"
He said
"Surely I have dominion.
And should I not take what I am given,
be it girl or gun?"

Friends are some the richer
—a kettle, a fleece or two—for the trick
they played: you in the grip of his ship on the Potomac

and your father months late
with the harvest canoe, ammunition
and bawling men that float for your ransom.

(These Englishmen your father captured wept upon their return
to bread and brandy, escaped back to his plenty. Small wonder,
you laugh, the way they went.)

1614, Spring

> [Pocahuntas, or Matoaka, the daughter of Powhatan, is married to an honest
> and discreet English gentleman, Master Rolfe on 5th April.]

Date written, there is no chronicler of place,
though the land has lungs and gives witness

to the flaccid white face of a man
you never should have known
who claims you as his own

progenitor
of those who scramble to your peoples' shores
rotted food stores the pit from which they emerge
as if from the earth.

[Rebecca Rolfe]

Crouching at your baptism, basin submerged,
you seek a rain of nations
the many suns that hang
over the favored earth.

But you walk past the place
where the living bells have rung,
body elsewhere. not in the geography
of the shipped, but proximate.
                              [This close:]

1619

Set loose, the English sails
that brought you to London
cross paths with a slave ship in the shoals.

               [The hold of history now, the throws of it.
               The rows of bodies now, a riotous wind]

Your skin recalls what it does not yet know:
This is not the whole of the story, not even
half. But it cannot be called back.

Grace Came for John Newton,

Author of "Amazing Grace"

1750

In this vessel's hold: ledgers, notes of sale and music, salve and salvation. My impoverished soul

1751

—flies. fever
flowering bodies.

1754

This was hour she first appeared, the goddess Grace to the Negress Briseis.
I could repeat the rhapsody she sang, for I have been richly and roundly paid.

—Amazing grace how sweet the sound that saved—

1769

"But suppose the blind man suddenly possessed of light."[1]

1780

Oh Lord of nations, "teach us how to die" how to abolish and abandon, free and forsake, pursue
parliament over pestilence— this dark millions in our midst.

1807

What monster gripped me (God or music?) and rescued me from bliss?

1754

Bruised, Briseis is back—

---

[1] John Newton. *The Christian Correspondent; or a Series of Religious Letters,
Written by the Rev. John Newton, ... to Captain Alexr. Clunie, ... Never Before Published.* (1790)

Girlhood and its Sorrows

for Elizabeth Hobbs Keckley and Mary Lincoln

1818

I was born
  attended by   a slave
   I am a mother myself now
 wife of a   coerced by a
  prominent White politician
    I have
  a taste for   a mind for
     material
 mint juleps, madeira wine   something about taking out
    the seams
 unravel me   on a dress, the cut of a neck
    my own matter
     reams of it
     like the paper-
thin muslin   that attests to my freedom
dress I married in   (like my husband claimed he was)

    I lived with him

 thirteen years   eight years
  maddened by the lamentable ways of men
 in a house dark with locusts   of plague
 tormented and wearing tulle.
 I cannot help but   I don't
    look back
  so they call me   for fear I'll become
   Lot's wife; a pillar of salt
      My former master said I was
      not worth my weight in

Despondent; I felt I could not   though I

                        work

                                    "supported seventeen people
                                    for two years five months."
            When I returned to the world after my son
Willie   George
        died, there was much wailing, wagging of tongues.
                None welcomed me but she.

The Mermaid of Charleston, 1867

I

A welcome wild, she gathered the people in front of Dr. Trott's apothecary shop just two years after the war. Some claimed they'd seen the reason for rain in her eyes, felt rumored fins; gills that went flap! as the *simbi* gulped the wind. In clutch of sin she'd been locked, rocked and cradled. Gin and gunpowder, jam and jelly; the store was no place for the sea-formed child in her belly. Pregnant, craving cornmeal, she stumbled, swore, tore into sacks of grain, meal, cherry pies.

Watched the slaughtered skies.

II

They dictated a letter to the city to him among them that could write. But the city, with its liturgy of logistics and White lies, advised that they drag the aqueous prisoner by her seaweed hair, hold a hearing in the public square. Ask of her crossly why she'd made herself known to the colored of Charleston when good White folks owned everything in sight? Had the might of meanness and militias and the sheer force of fright to fell whatever had cast her from the sea. How could she have made such an oversight? Such were the follies of Reconstruction days. Black gals, bold as brass and buxom, practically pushing delicate White ladies off public roads as they barreled towards the clapboard schools they'd made, humming offensively all the way... and now the mermaid...

III

Her flickering eyes and armored thighs. The flash of flesh, black as squid ink and unbridled, giving rise. She made them dream her bare, splayed on beds of moss green and spare; streaming hair fine as floss, once long, now shorn to mourn the lump of a baby she'd suddenly lost. New mothers sighed in sympathy as their paths crossed, whispering where they roamed, "No country road by which to lay the baby's bones." Others pursed their lips and said *please* "She gon' have to earn her keep like any woman. Work and weep."

IV

The people brought her frankincense and myrrh.

Love Root

Atlanta, 1881

Let the Cotton Expo come to Atlanta.
Let love-root run my tongue.

I will wander down Decatur
covered in women

striking
as he struck me once.

I won't wash clothes today
or next,

Will baptize neither sleeve
nor dress,

Only *behold!* This body
redressed.

Buttons from my high-laced neck
bare buttocks in the sun

Garment pooling
around my ankles—blue

as the dead they hung
in Jonesboro.

Declaration

with phrases from the Declaration of Independence

The body
Unalienable,
Truth self-evident, not
spoken of through possessives
"my hands, my feet," but, rather, through
what is:

Napé má núŋpa
two hands exist for me, these
arms upon which they're affixed
this chest, these lungs, this breath, gifts.
These breasts exist for me, not you.
These scars, too.

What was taken by deed and declaration,
"in the course of human events...." Now
returns. "Political bands," *Hunkpapa,*
Sicangu, "Connected with another"
Oglala. "Governments long
established" will endure.

Injure not her body
Unalienable,
Spoken and
What is.

We True Truants

We true truants renegade run into thought's thickets. Can't get you off my back-bridge. The brain, fickle and fixated, fried and feathered like a lynched woman watched. Listen, stop. Notice bark, bruise, bird. On a star line we cruise back to black and blessings unheard. Stage a failed return. I break the bound book and climb inside, discover the grace of governance: the scattered band, the people who rise. Garish guards at the walking place where we wish to arrive thrive like weeds, thickets that become California wildfires since settlers don't strategically burn as we true truants have learned must be done from mission citizens of Native nations that claim the land, and from thousand year old trees that [breathe] will not betray this bountiful burning, our plan.

I am the Fugitive Daughter of Your Eyes

for the women of Georgia State Penitentiary, 1909

There is no line
no stanza for me. I will die or not die
here. Poetry won't remember. I work.
I killed my father. I killed my father cuz
his hands were minefields I couldn't cross.
A firmament awaits me. I am the fugitive daughter
of your eyes. No one will recite "Daddy Daddy you bastard
I'm through" though he got me big with his. This is Georgia State Penitentiary.

It don't matter what you thought you knew. Don't matter if you pretty or plain or thick.
We all diggin' a ditch. Guards call us whores, say tomorrow they hangin' a witch
dress us in men's clothes as punishment. To imagine I'm a *him*. Stick
myself into any behind and get no time. Free as a bluebird, berry
pie; as rose-scented stanzas that walk, waltz, lope. I wonder
what it's like to talk sweet and low, salt the earth we still till,
own my time. A white woman worked here once; balked.
When the state came to save her, she acted mild.

They preach like we all a child of God but
some of us burn and some are lifted
from the fire. Since I'm worked
"like a I was a man" I'ma be
Shadrach, plan. No one
sings psalms for me,
writes poetry.

Harlem, 1912

Exiled east, she coupled with what cut,
became monument. This wasn't the Garden,
but glorious, lit. Here too were laws: his fists. Yet,
in Harlem, unhung tongues sung in truant throats
told the bliss of boys brung up wantless, strung just

Like instruments. He bellowed. Was big, high yellow.
Such a man as this could bastard her into light, wring
the necks of birds brighter than peonies, watch as she
peed, demand its direction, unreasonable speed. Dark
as she was why did they call this white slavery? It put

her in mind of sticky things: rich women's cake
iced too sweet melting in the North Carolina sun…
Mister above her in the sugared night, grunting a
woman's name with every unatoned thrust *"Evie
Evie, Oh lord! Eve"* swearing while she sky-stared

While she flailed—a cab, the rain, some too-
young goddess hailed—then tied him by
her hair-rope to their bedpost, slipped
her coat on, fled East of this man's
Eden to taste a Harlem night

Sweet. Just right.

Some Ellen

for Ellen Pryce / for Nana

Some Ellen touches
amber perfume to her skin

some Ellen with no
shortage of gin

dances in the woods
before the rebellion.

another still, captured by camera
on a street cobbled together by her laugh,

groceries about to spill,
descendants countless as shattered glass

heads home to feed her teeming ten
sweet milk and rice, then put them to bed,

place a plant on the windowsill
—its pane not yet broken by voices or vice—

a cool drink in the pitcher and
everything so newly citified, even

the stinking subway deemed "nice."
Ellen, north now

and all the richer.

Ally

Nawi, also called *James*, now called ancestor, did you whisper for great-grandmother's pleasure, "Yes, *Aglí Win*, Comes Home Woman," though her body descended from another continent? When you argued, did she gather her skirts about her, a shield of embroidered wildflowers? Raise her voice against domestic days, hours that seemed to mount like the risen bluffs of the *he sápa*? (Everything *mázaška ška iyá hi ya* those middling days of marriage, by the clock.) Did you let her win, knowing as you did that she was newly arrived; you were two decades her senior, with few skills, though you could farm hogs, and well? That you'd been marked by the census-taker who'd come to your door in 1900 a "ration Indian," when you were just twenty-four; unsure what the world, made new by English words like *plough* and *station,* might unfurl? In elder days, did you miss the cottonwood trees that blanket the northern earth? The sweet, tart things your mother used to make with chokecherries? When you first tasted your sweetheart's mustard greens and collards did you grin, grip great-grandma's netted hair, thick as Iktómi's web, dark and curled as *t at á ka hí ,* place your hands on her come-home hips, between which the baby's head emerged one day in July? Were you afraid: at once her father, yet so many miles from the land's heart, speaking a language that rendered you "*Sioux,*" meaning enemy, even though *Lakóta* means ally.

Pilot, 1935

Scene 1.

At least, at the very least, we had the movies. The dream makers: MGM and Universal, planetary and produced. In this one, a pilot lives in the guise of a girl. The setting is New York, 1924, and she is poor. Her favorite thing (besides cherry ices) is the glitter of the movies. In the picture house dark she gleams gap-toothed, brighter than the screen; more brilliant than Wall Street's mean dream; so bright that her skin is the scene. Where everybody wants to be.

Scene 2.

In the white folks' home where Pilot works, she is also the scene. Mrs. S _____, sadsmoking slip of a woman, shade of many mistresses, manages the minutiae of each unrelenting hour, meanders from bedroom to kitchen to shower, pretends not to watch sweat seep between cleavage as Pilot scrubs, arms sore. Then, like clockwork after her husband shuts the door, Mrs. S _____, lank and leering, discards her gown. Slaps frowns grabs begs. Wants to see how easy these country girls bed.

Scene 3.

1929 was flavored red. Grown men stripped naked and threw themselves from rooftops, making the pavement blush bashful. Pilot saw no difference; before the crash or after, the world still spun on its axis; her sweetheart was still hopelessly hers. When the doors of the Savoy Ballroom opened last year, hadn't he swung her high as the red planet above his head, promised they'd wed? Wasn't it he who'd first heard the music that played threateningly close to her throat, a saturnine song that sounded like the strangled notes of "no" ?

Scene 4.

In 1935, watching Oscar Micheaux's "Murder in Harlem," when Dorothy Van Engle's character is asked, "Do you work for white folks, honey, or colored?" Pilot replies, *"I work at the demand of daylight."* Silver screen's shadow, I walk willing into the cinematic dark to make my dwelling there. Starlet of street sweepers, darling to dozens of wilted wild working girls who perambulate, vie for a waif-like white house-wife to offer a living wage. In coming attractions watch me shine, take stage.

Scene 5.

When Mrs. S_____ caught Pilot trying on her clothes, she called her common country cunt, sent her back to the throng of gesturing black girls at 167th and Jerome in the Bronx, that region of souls saved by the Savoy. But it was there among the broken and brave, belittled and beautiful, that Pilot was seen. Newspaper women, colored like she, came. It wasn't a movie set for a star, but they looked through lenses at her eyes' dark, saw floundering flight, her daddy's dying might, and the guise she lived under: born a girl, but really Pilot of storms.

It's Hard to Explain

It's hard to explain it, what it's like in this skin
the blonde smokes her cigarette and she murmurs "thin gin."

It's hard to explain it, why she burned my arm,
then traipsed to the kitchen
where she rang the alarm

Why I first mopped her floor,
Then I crawled toward the door
and I buried, at last, her sparrow.

Work

legs splayed (instruments? do they sound?) an exchange behind the dark at the movies that time i want $10 for it because i looked for myself and didn't see you. i want ten dollars ($10) or i'll hide in the paper place where you won't find me i am dark enough.

i am already broke so get inside me i implore you.
there was panic at daybreak that the world would not be remade if cotton was not caressed it must be touched just right.

you can trace the back of the woman you shamed but she is not done being made. "this is the occasion for her undoing" you think and release the trellises of time so that she might grow toward you but her back (the bitch black) breaks and the wind swallows her and gives the rest of her edible parts to those who will feed.

no such thing as close only leaving close behind. so many boats anchored to so many shores. so many things float in water.

Dilate.

I wake up at night and don't know how I ended up here,
feet flags of surrender unfurled, my husband gone. I don't know
where the child I gave birth to went, which way the bathroom is. I want
the nurse to stop whispering *"tomorrow, tomorrow she will die of this"* as if I cannot
hear her, as if tomorrow is not just another terrifyingly ordinary day, marked not by time
but temperament (if and when I can manage it) as if I don't know
my husband won't mourn me, doesn't touch me,
and when he does his eyes are closed
and he is saying, "tomorrow."

Untimely Ripped

I was not born, but untimely ripped.
No telling what I may destroy:
desire's black root, it's bulbous tip;
the noise of burning trees moving
toward your ardent castle.

Within its walls, I beckon
and obey; slay, finally, the pall
you cast over my dreams; eat
at the mouth of plentiful horn.

No navel, no cord
only the smooth expanse of flesh
that marks me motherless.

Gone to Ninevah

What is expected of us, epoch? Huge asses, Helens,
all. And the future of this industry of hips?

Another loathsome sea
another ship
that casts off the bodies of she
            (there were three)
whose god the boatswain feared
lest it sink, weight
of another Jonah descended into blue,

gone

to Ninevah
where they no longer say,
"she shall be stoned for this," but instead,
"you want to give me all that—

come"

to a place where she can be redone.
only the parts that matter: breast and heart
shaped

(w)hole.

Pie

he said he'd cook dinner,
you'd go for a walk.

unexpected, then
you turned around with skirt down
and him behind

you resigned,
having pushed him from you twice
with a fair amount of force

these past six years,
since you were sixteen and he
forty-five, one of the many men
who called you Pie, because you were "sweet as"
with sweat sharp to the taste, like cherries.

when you'd gone to the movies
you'd liked it enough. he'd bought
popcorn and asked for your underwear,
which you'd given, wet.

later, he said, *"you're a big strong girl*
you're a big strong girl" and you assented,
though you'd felt a bit like a horse

rocking beneath him, as taught.

now, caught in the colossus of it all
he takes you by force, felling your first
architecture of desire

and you are someplace on fire asking
for an end to this country of men,
spun to river
waded
washed.

Phaedra's Love

Let me not be a foreigner everywhere. Let me build my house somewhere. Not in my mother's wild womb. There are too many horses there. Perhaps in you? You always were so very kind. Never bound me like the others did. Never
robbed me blind.

Leda's Daughters

God the swan
came dressed in heather,
a long necked someone
at the door, feathers
on the floor.

"Will you not stay awake with me, sister?" We,
not Helen and Clytemnestra, but lesser sisters hatched
recall a night we were roused by guards.

You find fabric, patches of our father's neck,
black and white, business casual, that speak
of a woman in charge, who moves swift and bright
as a wing through the workplace.

Mother, Leda,
I wish they'd burned the hallway where it happened.
where you slid in grief and father stood above you,
unsure how to hold your human hand.

I wish they'd burned it,
feathers, fingernail clippings
and all.

Gethsemane raised,
you return each time to swans.

Helios Child

for Summer

In alabaster halls
sit rows of black folks' shoes.

Shoes of those who've
come and gone; shoes of those
who don't have none

who walk on concrete
in burning sun.

On Helios' neck
by laces hang hundreds
of poor folks' clanging shoes.

Here below, his forgotten child
slips singed feet into shoals, where

footprints fossilize; become the shade
of a people whose children played
whose laughter —once— was grace.

Iphigenia at Birmingham, 1963

for four girls, victims of the 16th Street Baptist Church bombing

This was the most remarkable thing:
so many hands.

Hands that silken burning hair,
lay on sacred scalps

Hands that circle like young suns
around the necks of birds wrung for auspice

Passing the collection basket,
basking in Sunday glory, hands

Won't scrub, for once, the
white-tiled houses of the unholy.

Bedecked and blessed, palms open
hymnals, hunt their sacrificial calf.

      Then a perfectly ordered moment at last:

Mild wind on a nearby hillside, cool
balm for the blistering child, stirs like sin.

Matchstick-thin, set on fire by klansmen,
four girls may walk again in myth. But here

in Birmingham, the promised deer
of Artemis does not appear;

She who carries the offering wood
is also the body made myriad.

See: the articulated spine of history
then the brutal base of today's

Temple of girlhood wants:
new shoes in grown girl blue

To eat ices that turn tongues red
rub the shine off foreheads

Lie asleep in a room of girls
tell mama not to weep

Meet cousins in Carolina
taste the yellow honey of bees.

Pax Animalis

Wolf-headed,
I wake the wee hours.
Nothing worries me.
My babies cling to my teats.

Soon all roads will be raised
by story from the dead.

Order my bones and make of them ruins.
Order my bones and make of them—-

The peace of animal. A mountain of amphorae,
broken, that becomes the heart.

The Haruspex

Sometimes I'm so lonely I could spit.
Lonely for the radio on Sunday mornings
and for something to split
the animal's gut
when the Haruspex cuts.

"Why were we thrown together?"
I'd ask its entrails. "And
why not thrown close?"

I guess if fresh blood then "yes"
the reply. "You're fit for travel,
fit to form." But what of the skin
the haruspex leaves behind?

And what of my household,
what of it when?

Wild Flag

orphan

tell me what you know about collectivity. run
run
run 'til brightness bit-breaks

over the tracks and something is saved. ephemera: a piece of this, a ribbon
of that, and (archivable) a photo of you, before you were abandoned to history you were held,
infant. "this ismyfavoritething." this

swaddling before burning children
like cannons through a wild flag.

Helen of the Swamplands

I.

Nights I whisper to the swampland reeds. curse my ancient name, evade her wanton whispers, wander close. If I leave you here, your densely coiled hair a helmet against the dawn bombs, you'll be a baby among the bulrushes. The thrush! of it, the reeds I would split

th e thr ust of him, brows knit.

II.

She of the big house is averse to the damp, but booted, in her bustle crams the curled strands spotted while hunting those who flee swamplands:

III.

Me, first and foremost, favored of the flighted gods.

After Her Eyes

for an unidentified subject of Louis Agassiz

The daguerreotype
phonetically sounds like
the type of dog used to hound the truant (she who ran

towards the church of the woods before it was torched after Nat Turner's rebellion, wept over the ordered graves of women who had, in life, been intractable, then returned. Not to the evergreen forests of pastoral poems, but to the ever-hungry need of children, the fabric of whose lives she had time only at night to rend and sew, whose bodies she prayed would mend, grow.)

But no. It is an image
fearfully and wonderfully made,
plate by gleaming plate. Now
an archival sliver,
then by silver.

Those born on the dark continent
he asks to undress, gaze direct
at the lens, demure not
demon, but her eyes

seek the Garden.
sac the town.

Backbone of the New South

She concentrates, teases out
the knots in the light until
it's practically hide,
tanned and supple.

Winter but braless and why
shouldn't she be?
Hours at this and such
little progress: a crease

in the sheet long as a spine
(The spine split first then
his head on her shirt)
her husband his—*huh*

splattered on the walls of her home
never on the whites
of their hoods.

The blood she wouldn't
clean just now,
as that was the last of him
the rest in the ground.

The Widow's Oil

she'd poured over his feet.
a trifle for her debt, really
the night drawn and quartered

      instead of flesh unseamed in day's heat

owl even answering when the vessel brimmed, broke
and she'd cursed, called on Elisha in hope.

Shared Crop

She'd buried you herself.

Your unprodigal daughter,
face plain; not dressed
with paint or drenched
by tears. (She could not
spare the salt. It cost 5¢
a paltry quarter-pound). This
was the measure of her years:
weight of prayers spent on kin,
weight of prayers you kept, sweet-wrapped,
like the chocolate stash of a child still in swaddling clothes.
After the burial they were shoved and stowed, the precious things
you, debt-free, owned. The wheelbarrow you'd borrowed come freedom was listed on his ledger.
You'd shared each harvest for worse or better, in sickness and health. By stealth he'd feasted on
your garden's bounty, secreted glances of your daughter's hair... your daughter for whom you
couldn't even buy a new dress for a bargain fair. The months after jubilee had fled so fast that
you could not grasp the mounting debt. Yet she'd worn the dress her mother made

To bury you herself.

Pearl

Child who ran from the grin and glitter of Baptist gods (gas, guns) you are, at 20, rarely seen without a beer, blaspheme in your Texas town. Forsaken though you surely are, a hymn limns your hitchhiked way to California, and you pray for a smoother ride, a Mercedes Benz, maybe a gauntlet with which to grab guys who give female travelers grief, a guide. Your soul like an animal wakes early to pelt stones at those who look, then coos "come close, honey," gathers morning—damp sheets around itself like Aphrodites' waves. Crested, your voice is a feast, offering of a country that sells small mementoes (the beads from your garments) to men who have called you Pearl, but never given a string, men to whom you whisper "welcome home," who finish fast, discard the high, heavy hull of your head, lank hair. Your corpus lands where you've sung the body, cloaked and pitted, flesh from soul riven, gone the color of Levi's and of rain.

The Sounding Field

Sound plenitude, restore me to the field of enunciation. Welcome lovers to my marriage bed hewn of holly, wood akin to that which Penelope should have burned after Odysseus, under hood, returned to interrupt her sojourns in the flowering field of thought. She, home and hearth's heathen excess. Her hedon heart an emergence place for the world's first sound, a cry for word, for water. What did sex sound like before discourse? Before we sanctified and damned? Like wood burning winsome as the wild caught aflame? Like Penelope's own arrows maiming the hearts of men? Was it pitiless, too much the color red? Red behind the angered eye, wine-dark as the sea Odysseus rode toward Penelope's serpentine soul. Was this our crime? That we mined the sky for the words to describe "close" and "warn" and "want," stripped it bare, then sounded a death knell, learned the words "woman" and "hell."

Lakota Grammar

I.

This is what the language teaches, waúnspemakhiye:
Do not be ashamed that you misunderstood possessives.
That you were not a thing to be taken and torn, but a verb:
Winyan, "I am a woman." That everything in Lakótiyapi is,
can be a verb. Not parts of speech but a series of doings:

I walked away that morning. I said, "this cannot happen again."
I sat in the sanctuary at the mission school that summer. I thought
'I was raped.'
I looked at the stained glass windows and saw
the language saves.

héya wachekiye.

In the settlers' tongue, I did not speak of it, but mumbled each morning
a prayer in Lakótiyapi before the work was begun, the work of how to say
"Inside" and "outside" in relation. Of how to intone to one another,
"Taŋyáŋ ómani ye." Have a good journey.
How to say both "sweetgrass" and "street."

II.

Wonder of the emergence place in its vibrant verdure, almost singing
with what you have lost: the generations, your father's voice, how the
funeral home feared they would not be able to break the frozen earth
to bury him, that you'd have to return in the spring... all these things.

The one you mean to learn is his grandfather James' language,
James, born just before chokecherry season, who left the place
of his beginnings to farm hogs in Polk County, who taught your
father a new tradition: to sweat in a makeshift lodge in the yard.

Where there are no relatives there is poetry, paltry and pitiful
to the last. It is with you in the cave of your beginnings, scatters
you all over when you expected to be whole, expected to live
in a house made not of paper but of hide, on whose tanned side
you would paint the deeds that make you woman.

III.

"Wayáčhi kta he?"
"Wačhípi uŋmáspe šni."
But you can. Dance, too, is a language you understand:
bellowing bones against the floor, pelvis making its own sacred mountain,
the scarf you tie around your waist a prayer flag.

IV.

When the pilgrims leave there's been no progress, only the flag
of a forsaken nation on the face of the moon, only the steel of the city
you were born into crying for itself as the land claims it, claims you, hokščhaŋlkiyapi.

After the Flood

mitochondrial
mother sews shut
her womb

thread made of sinew
what animal
has she

parted with for such
illumed bone
needle

such red thread with which
to unmake us
again

an ark's aperture
then, a storm of
numbers

torrential twoness
terrifying.
behold

flesh this floating thing
has made live and
let die

tepid mouth of sea.
how the ark parts
bodies

from crown to crotch.
the helmsman knew.
bargained not

with God. only stored
grain, watched for the
promised rain— perfect
in its plainness, like a
tender
new
math.

Vivarium

They'd built a boat, clawed its anchor from an angel's moat—
experience enough for an ecosystem apart
perhaps a private moon
to cast over their fears
of scanty harvest;
not enough air;
the goat (unclean)
missing its cloven-footed pair.
Noah they kept in verdant lair, captured but
not constrained, skin cooling beneath the biosphere's rod
far from his burning god, nothing to do but compare cubits,
count the yieldless rib.

Ruin

She is self-righteous and assured. I am fulminant. First
time he said, "I love you" it was in the backseat of Ruin.
I said, "I don't know. I need to ride down Main to determine
the angle at which stars meet hollow." I seek the guide of Ruin.
My parents, too, said "I love you." I am body, at home in my frame,
laden by books in other languages (Russian, Latin). I pack my bag
with things I can't possibly carry. Appear harried, heave at the exam's first
page. Boy, with you I am undone, don clothes from decades past (kitten heels),
squeal, "Call me Donna Reed." Joined as if in vein, by vertebrae, my sistermother
laughs, "We're not animal people." We are animal. Gutted, her girl is gone. She wraps
her sash against the cold and retreats. This is a gift for me. She was fifteen, my father
coy. And I am an envoy to the saints. One night each year they stumble in their star shoes
at this town fair, cottoncandy-winged. I, Donna Reed again to them, welcome heavenly hosts.
They're here for Ruin, rapture's ropes. When they get drunk off earth things, this town will be
First.

Inhabit

To wake,
discover
a space being
inhabits your shoes
feathered and plumed
that someone's assumed
your human form; your name

still, you must perform; are on stage.
for what else but this are you paid?
once, you were given trinkets for your
child skin, your winning smile, by a petty,
managerial deity, who filed them under,
"not person," but pauper "not a feast,"
but the priest that keeps
wafer safe; wine in case;
Negress in her place
not to break
or be broken
until the 'I'
presents itself.
I, singing.
I, unslain.

Aureole

The checkout girl at the co-op in Gallup
is comprised of a concentrated light. She
washes her hands, once, twice, three times,
wrings them dry.

Out back she watches fires take the trash.
We are both despised; poor women, brown
as sand or coffee ground to its last elixir.

Once she was chrysalis.
There were horses then.

Amen.

Opening the book, I find a first circulation date: December 15th, 1977. That year, stars gave themselves for a poor girl's Christmas tree, the brightest lights the Bronx had ever seen.

Now, sitting in the place opened by that page my cousin says, "I didn't know how time worked until I was 33, and then it was only in moments like these, sharing bread before we burn all that our grandmother didn't take with her; that is, a flurry of photographs, the measure of this minute, our mothers' mean miracles, and hers. This is the promise of ashes, of the priest whose assured thumb crosses as if on a street to say, 'You'll return here.'"

be my body for me

But they want to hear her sing it;
stand in the ruins and sing, finally
a bluebird.

Invite the chorus to keen,
gladdened at the wreck they see,
buoyant in the waters of applause.

Nakedness' curtain
must be re-drawn;
pants and pasties
cost extra to own.

For this task a daughter is raised:
"be my body for me,
cradle to grave."

More from the Washington Writers' Publishing House

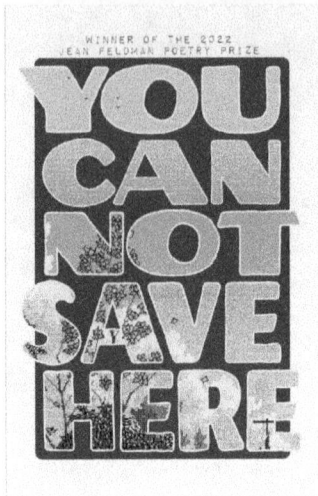

You Cannot Save Here
Tonee (Anthony) Moll

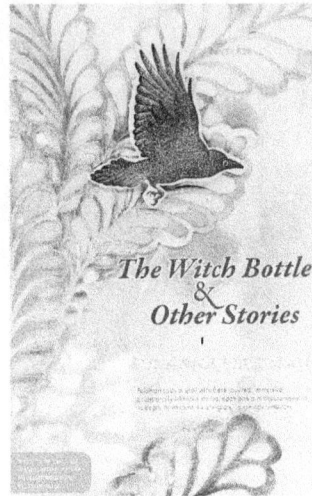

The Witch Bottle
& Other Stories
Suzanne Feldman

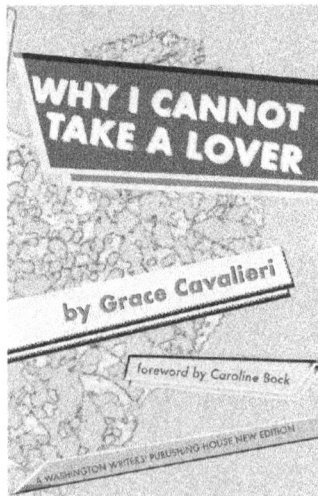

Why I Cannot
Take a Lover
Grace Cavalieri

Altamira
Myra Sklarew

MSAC
maryland state arts council

PROUD MEMBER
[clmp]
COMMUNITY OF LITERARY MAGAZINES & PRESSES
WWW.CLMP.ORG

DC COMMISSION on the ARTS & HUMANITIES

Washington Writers' Publishing House

Washington Writers' Publishing House (WWPH) is an independent, nonprofit, cooperative press founded in 1975. Our mission is to publish and celebrate writers from DC, Maryland, and Virginia. To learn more about our fiction, poetry, and creative nonfiction manuscript contests, our bi-weekly literary journal, *WWPH Writes*, and to purchase more WWPH books, please visit:

www.washingtonwriters.org

Follow us on:
Twitter: @wwphpress
Facebook: @WWPH
Instagram: @writingfromWWPH

Contact us at:
wwphpress@gmail.com

Sign up for our bi-weekly, online literary journal, *WWPH Writes*, by scanning the QR Code on the right. Free to subscribe and free to submit. Emails are only twice a month. Be part of the Washington Writers' Publishing House community, the (almost) 50-year-old cooperative, nonprofit literary press based in our nation's capital.

9781941551349